The Steptoe and Son Encyclopedia

Brian Carver

Contents

Introduction

Steptoe and Son is a classic British sitcom that ran on the BBC between 1962-74.

The series has two iconic characters – Albert Steptoe and his rag and bone man son Harold. Wildred Brambell as Albert and Harry H. Corbett as Harold both give wonderful performances in the series.

As well as being a great comedy, Steptoe and Son has many dramatic elements and social commentary relating to the relationship between father and son, changes in society, their working class existence and their rather old fashioned rag and bone trade.

Find out more about this iconic series in this Encyclopedia.

The Encyclopedia

A

Adverts

In 1977 Harry H. Corbett and Wilfrid Brambell appeared in British advertisements for Ajax cleaning products. Two ads were made and they were filmed in Australia during a tour.

In 1981 they filmed another British tv ad, this time for Kenco Coffee. This was their last appearance together as Steptoe and Son.

And Afterwards At...

And Afterwards At... is an episode of Steptoe and Son. It was first shown on the 4th October 1965. It is the 1st episode of series 4.

Harold is getting married to Melanie. will it go to plan?

Also stars George A. Cooper as Uncle Arthur, Rose Hill as Auntie May, Joan Newell as Aunt Ethel, Mollie Sugden as the bride's mother,

Karol Hagar as Melanie, Robert Webber as the Vicar, Rita Webb as Auntie Freda, Gretchen Franklin as Aunt Daphne, Fred Hugh as First Man, Leslie Sarony as Melanie's father, George Tovey, George Hirste and Betty Cardno.

Harold is going to marry at last - although he is planning to carry on living at the house with Albert. When Melanie decides to not go through with the wedding at the Church Harold is upset, but Albert is pleased that the status quo can be resumed. This one has a bigger than usual cast featuring the Steptoe clan.

And So to Bed

And So to Bed is an episode of Steptoe and Son. It was first broadcast on the 7th September 1974. It is the 2nd episode of series 8.

Harold's girlfriend is not impressed with his dirty old bed, so he buys a new one - a water one!

Also features Lynn Farleigh as Marcia and Angus MacKay as Salesman.

This is a good late episode. Harold again has

to deal with a snooty salesman who looks down on him when making a purchase. And of course it was obvious what was going to happen to the water bed and what Albert was going to do to it.

Any Old Iron

Any Old Iron is an episode of Steptoe and Son. It is the 3rd episode in series 5 and was first broadcast on the 20th March 1970.

An elderly cultured antiques dealer - Timothy - visits the Steptoes. Harold sees the chance to have an intellectual friend who will help him open an antiques shop. But Timothy is gay and interested in more than friendship.

Also features Richard Hurndall as Timothy Stanhope, Valerie Bell as Dolly Miller and Roger Avon as the Policeman.

This is not very politically correct but wonderful episode with Harold seemingly unaware of the gay man's interest in him. Albert tries to warn him, only to be told that he has "poof mania" by Harold!

Argent

Douglas Argent (1921-2010) was a British director and producer who produced and directed series 8 of Steptoe and Son.

His other work includes Till Death Do Us Part,The Liver Birds, Q8 and Q9, Never the Twain and Fawlty Towers.

He was born in Bexleyheath.

B

Back in Fashion

Back in Fashion is an episode of Steptoe and Son. It was first broadcast on the 31st August 1974. It is the first series of series 8.

A photographer wants to use the Steptoes' yard as a location for a fashion shoot with some attractive models.

Also features Madeline Smith as Carol, Roy Holder as the photographer, Peter Birrel as the agent, Michael Earl as policeman, Ava Cadell, Christine Donna, Sally Farmiloe, Claire Russel, Hazel Wilson.

A very farcical episode of Steptoe with the models thinking Harold is blind due to his sunglasses, and Albert looking through the keyholes and even the ceiling to get a look at the models undressing. Of course Harold sees the chance to be a model, but Albert is asked and is a success.

The Bath

The Bath is an episode of Steptoe and Son. It was first broadcast on the 10th January 1963. It is the 2nd episode of series 2.

Harold wants a normal bath - he is fed up with the tin one they use in the living room. He attempts to build one in Albert's room. When Harold brings round a girlfriend, Albert has a bath in the tin bath in the living room.

This episode also stars Yootha Joyce as Delilah, Harold's girlfriend, and Marjie Lawrence as Martine.

A great episode where Albert embarrasses Harold as usual disrupting his love life with his slovenly behaviour.

Bear

The bear seen in the Steptoes' lounge was a real stuffed bear.

After the series ended it resided at Mr Potter's Museum of Curiosities at Jamaica Inn on Bodmin Moor. The museum sold the bear in 2003. It can now be seen at the Museum of Comedy at Bloomsbury Way in London.

Bell

Valerie Bell is a British actress who appears in 3 episodes of Steptoe and Son. In The Bird (1962) she plays Roxanne. In Any Old Iron? (1970) she plays Dolly Miller. In The Party (1973) she plays a party guest.

She appears widely in British television in the 60s and 70s in programmes such as Benny Hill, The Avengers, Armchair Theatre, The Saint, Z Cars and The Sweeney.

Her film roles include Secrets of a Door-to-Door Salesman (1973) and Crossplot (1969).

Bird

Norman Bird (1924-2005) was a British actor. He appears in two episodes of Steptoe and Son: Without Prejudice (1970) where he plays the head of the Residents' Association, and Men of Property (1970) where he plays the Bank Manager.

A prolific character actor, he appears many film and television productions.

His television work includes Fawlty Towers, Rising Damp, Department S, Ever Decreasing Circles, Worzel Gummidge, and Hammer House of Mystery and Suspense.

His film roles include The League of Gentlemen (1960), Victim (1961), Maniac (1963), Young Winston (1972), The Medusa Touch (1978), Omen III: The Final Conflict (1981).

Bird was born in Coalville in Leicestershire.

The Bird

The Bird is an episode of Steptoe and Son. It was first aired on the 14th June 1962. It is the first episode from series 1.

Harold is attached to a woman and wants to bring her back to meet his father. But Albert is determined to scupper the relationship, and uses his usual brand of tricks to do so.

This episode features Valerie Bell as Roxanne, Harold's girlfriend.

Another episode where Albert spoils things for Harold. When Harold's girlfriend is late, Albert takes pleasure in teasing Harold about it, and when she turns up late, Harold slams the door in his face. We then find that horrible Albert has put the clock forward to trick Harold into thinking his girlfriend is late, which is a typical Albert.

The Bonds That Bind Us

The Bonds That Bind Us is an episode of Steptoe and Son. It was first broadcast on the 11th February 1964. It is the 6th episode of series 3.

Albert wins £1000 on the Premium Bonds. He refuses to share the money with Harold (because Harold sold his share of the bonds to Albert previously) and goes on a spending spree and smartens up his image, and takes a girlfriend Madge who is interested in his new wealth.

Also features June Whitfield as Madge.

It is interesting to see Albert cleaned up in this one! And course he goes on a pending spree after gaining some money which he does several times in the series.

A Box in Town

A Box in Town is an episode of Steptoe and Son. It was first shown on the 1st November 1965. It is the 5th episode of series 4.

Harold brings a girlfriend back to the house, but Harold refuses to go to bed. Harold then decides to get a bachelor pad - an attic bedsit flat.

Also stars Yootha Joyce as Avis, Majorie Rhodes, Freda Bamford, Annie Leake, and Hilda Barry.

Another episode where Harold tries to have some independence and it is not too successful. Ironically Albert uses the fact that Harold is not in the house to entertain some women.

Brambell

Wilfrid Brambell (1912-72) was an Irish actor. He is one of the leads in the Steptoe and Son, playing Albert Steptoe.

Brambell's film roles include The Quatermass Experiment (1953), Where the Bullets Fly (1966), Witchfinder General (1968), A Hard Day's Night (1964), Crooks in Cloisters (1964), Alice in Wonderland (1966), Carry On Again Doctor (1969), Holiday on the Buses (1973), Sword of the Valiant (1984) as Porter, The Terence Davies Trilogy (1983)

His other television roles include Just William, All Creatures Great and Small, Never Say Die, Oh Brother!, Armchair Theatre and Citizen James and Nineteen Eighty-Four

He had many theatre roles, including as landlord as Rooksby in Eric Chappell's The Banana Box - this was later adapted as the television sitcom Rising Damp.

Early on in his career he had several roles as older men, and this led to him being cast as Albert Steptoe who was older than Brambell: he was 49 in 1962 13 years older than Harry H. Corbett. The casting of a character actor as Albert (as well as Harry H. Corbett) allowed the series to have convincing dramatic scenes as well as the usual farce seen in a comedy sitcom.

Brambell was born in Dublin. He worked as a reporter for The Irish Times before becoming an actor at The Gate Theatre in Dublin. He joined the British forces entertainment group ENSA during WWII. After the war he gained roles in British television and film. He went on to be a prolific character actor.

He had some problems in his personal life due to his homosexuality. He died of cancer aged 72 in London in 1985.

C

Christmas Night with the Stars

Brambell and Corbett appeared on the BBC's Christmas variety show Christmas Night with the Stars on 1962 and 1967.

In 1962 they played the Steptoes in a sketch written by Galton and Simpson. No copies of the sketch are available.

In 1967 they again performed in the show in a

short filmed sketch written by Galton and Simpson. This still exists.

Clackett

Dolly Clackett is a local girl who Harold often dates. She is mentioned several times in the series - but never actually seen.

The Colour Problem

The Colour Problem is an episode of Steptoe and Son. It is the 5th episode of series 5. It was first broadcast on the 3rd April 1970.

Harold wants to buy a sports car to impress his girlfriend Muriel. But Albert wants a colour television to replace their old black and white one.

Also features Anthony Sharp as the Doctor, Geoffrey Adams as a Policeman and Carmel Cryan as Muriel.

Harold is determined to buy his car so he can have some fun with his girlfriend. But after he does so Albert goes missing and ends up in hospital with amnesia. He again uses illness to get his way and make Harold feel guilty.

Come Dancing

Come Dancing is an episode of Steptoe and Son. It is the 2nd episode of series 6. It was first broadcast on the 9th November 1970.

The colour version of this episode is available.

Harold wants to woo a woman who is a big fan of ballroom dancing; but Harold can't dance. Albert teaches him.

Also features Tony Melody as the Milkman.

A classic episode with Albert showing off another of his talents - dancing. Although this time it does not work out for Harold with the twist ending: Harold has been taught the women's steps.

Cooper

George A. Cooper (1925-) is an English actor. He appears in 2 episodes of Steptoe and Son: And Afterwards (1965) and Oh What a Beautiful Morning (1972) where he appears as Uncle Arthur.

Born in Yorkshire, Cooper has had many roles in television and film such as Dracula Has

Risen From the Grave (1968), Bless This House (1972), Tom Jones (1963), Grange Hill, Some Mothers Do Ave Em The Avengers, Doctor Who and The Saint. He also worked in theatre.

Corbett

Harry H. Corbett OBE (1925-1982) was a British actor. He is one of the leads in Steptoe and Son with his role as Harold Steptoe.

His other television roles include: The Adventures of Robin Hood, Theatre 70, Studio 4, The Edgar Wallace Mystery Theatre, Mr Aitch, Armchair Theatre, The Best Things in Life, Potter and Tales From the Unexpected.

His film roles include Ladies Who Do (1963), The Big Day (1960), The Bargee (1964), The Sandwich Man (1966), Carry on Screaming! (1966), The Magnificent Seven Deadly Sins (1971), Percy's Progress (1974), Hardcore (1977), Jabberwocky (1977), Silver Dream Racer (1980).

He worked widely in the theatre - Corbett was a student of Stanislavski's system.

Corbett was born in Burma. He moved to

Manchester to live with his aunt when he was 18 months old. He served with the Royal Marines in WWII. After the war Corbett trained as a radiographer before taking up acting. He used the name Harry H. Corbett as there was already a Harry Corbett in the showbiz world - the Sooty puppeteer.

Early in his career he plays tough characters due to his brooding looks. He was called "England's Marlon Brando".

Galton and Simpson decided to cast him as Harold Steptoe in their one off play The Offer in 1962. This was the start of Corbett's iconic role.

Corbett said:

"I had met Galton and Simpson and told them how much I admired their work, and I really did, and I said to them if they ever felt I could work with them then...well, I never envisaged in a thousand years going into light entertainment. I looked at what was on television and the only thing making any, I don't know, social comment was the Hancocks, the Eric Sykes, this kind of half hour comedy programme, you see. And ooh, I did envy them. Anyway, they remembered this conversation, clearly, and this thing about the rag and bone men thumped through the door. I read it, and immediately wired back - 'delicious, delighted, can't wait to work on it".

Corbett was known as a serious actor, but his role in the popular Steptoe and Son meant that he was typecast as a more comic actor. Some have suggested that this ruined his career, but he still had varied roles after his casting as Steptoe, although Corbett accepted that the role changed the nature of his acting career.

Corbett died aged only 57 of a heart attack in 1982.

Crossed Swords

Crossed Swords is an episode of Steptoe and Son. It was first shown on the 11th October 1965. It is the 2nd episode of series 4.

Harold buys a Meissen porcelain figurine. An antiques dealer offers £250, but he decides to auction it to get a better price. The Steptoes try and raise the bidding price themselves at the auction.

Also stars Derek Nimmo as Antique Shop Proprietor, Basil Dignam, Mark Singleton,

Ralph Nossek, Tim Buckland, Philip Howard, William Raynor, Frank Littlewood and Peter Thompson.

A fun episode - typical of Galton and Simpson's writing. Here Harold again does a bit of bad business because of his greed and incompetence in trying to raise the price of the figurine at the auction.

Cuckoo in the Nest

Cuckoo in the Nest is an episode of Steptoe and Son. It was first broadcast on the 21st December 1970 and is the 8th and last episode of series 6.

The colour version of this episode survives.

Albert's long lost Australian son Arthur turns up. Albert pampers him giving him money and allowing him not to work even though he is given a share of the company. Harold becomes jealous.

Also stars Kenneth J. Warren as Arthur and Edwin Brown as Taxi Driver.

Albert is not very nice to Harold here spoiling Arthur whilst Harold has to work hard. Again

Harold leaves and sets up his own business and is not a great success.

The Curse of Steptoe

The Curse of Steptoe is a television play about the making of Steptoe and Son and the relationship between Corbett and Brambell. It was first shown in 2008 on BBC4.

Jason Isaacs played Harry H. Corbett, and Phil Davis played Wilfrid Brambell. The writer was Brian Frills.

The play shows the lives and relationship of the actors during the duration of the television series. It shows how Corbett was typecast and unable to find work outside of Steptoe and Son, even though he was a talented actor before taking the part. Brambell's private life with his alcoholism and homosexuality are also depicted.

The Curse of Steptoe gained great reviews and viewing figures. But there were complaints from Corbett's family and Galton and Simpson that the play was not a truthful depiction of Corbett and Bramble.

Galton and Simpson said:

"during this entire period [that the series was made] we were unaware of any conflict between the actors save from the occasional gritting of Wilfrid's false teeth when Harry had the perceived audacity to give him a little direction. At all other times they were the acme of professionalism."

We didn't recognise any of that. Really didn't. Any notion of friction or hatred between Corbett and Brambell was inaccurate. They worked beautifully together."

Harry H. Corbett's nephew said:

"the drama was inaccurate and defamatory. In addition to numerous factual errors, he two actors did not hate each other, and that the suggestion that Steptoe and Son ruined either actor's career was nonsense."

Because of complaints, the BBC revised the play twice on repeats - once by 23 seconds, and then by 69 seconds. A disclaimer was shown at the start:

"The following drama is inspired by the lives of real people. For the purpose of the narrative some events have been invented or conflated."

The BBC Trust Editorial Standards Committee subsequently stated that the play did not conform to Fairness and Accuracy guidelines because of the inaccurate depictions of Corbett and Brambell. The DVDs of the play were withdrawn.

D

A Death in the Family

A Death in the Family is an episode of Steptoe and Son. It is the first episode of series 5.

The Steptoes' horse Hercules dies and they buy a new horse. Unfortunately they did not release that the new horse is a female and that she is pregnant. The new horse is named Hercules II.

A sad episode as it involves the death of the Steptoes' beloved horse.

The Desperate Hours

The Desperate Hours is an episode of Steptoe and Son. It is the 7th and last episode of series 7. It was first broadcast on the3rd April

1972.

Harold and Albert are trying to keep warm on a winter's night, struggling to find money for the electricity meter and with no food. Two convicts escape from the nearby prison and decide to stay at the Steptoes for the night.

Also features Leonard Rossiter as Johnny Spooner and J.G. Devlin as Frank Ferris.

One of the classic episodes of Steptoe and Son. The Steptoes are really poor in this one paying the electricity meter with foreign coins and with only some cold porridge and old cheese to eat. The prisoners say they get much better treatment in prison. And of course the prisoners' relationship with each other with a young one and an old one mirrors the Steptoes' relationship.

The Diploma

The Diploma is an episode of Steptoe and Son. It was first broadcast on the 5th July 1962. It is the 5th episode from Series 1.

Harold decides to learn a new trade to escape the rag and bone trade so tries to get a diploma in television repair. Of course Albert ruins his plans.

Harold tries to better himself, but as usual Albert knows more about the topic and ultimately spoils Harold's plans. A familiar scenario in the series.

Divided We Stand

Divided We Stand is an episode of Steptoe and Son. It is the 6th episode in series 7. It was first broadcast on the 17th March 1972.

Harold wants to redecorate, but argues with Albert. He then decides to partition the house so they both have separate parts!

This is probably the most famous episode of Steptoe and Son and is a classic. Harold's partition of the house, with his part more cultures, poses practical problems with half the appliances such as the cooker and tv on each side of the partition. And the old communist East German feel is complete with the turnstile that has to be used to access each others part of the property.

Dodd

Brambell and Corbett appeared on The Ken Dodd Show in 1966. This BBC show featured a live performance on stage of the Steptoes on Blackpool beach. A recording still exists.

E

The Economist

The Economist is an episode of Steptoe and Son. It was first broadcast on the 28th June 1962. It is the 3rd episode from Series 1.

Harold has an interest in economics and tries to teach Albert about bulk buying. But his purchases of false teeth and gas masks are not successful.

This episode also stars Frank Thornton as a seller.

A laboured early episode in which Harold's business schemes are a failure. This theme would be revisited several times in the series.

Episodes

58 episodes of Steptoe and Son were made. There are 8 series, with 3 specials.

The first episode was a Comedy Playhouse one off called The Offer. This as first shown on 5th January 1962.

Series 1 has 5 episodes. It was aired between 14th June 1962 and 12th July 1962.

The episodes in the series are:

1- The Bird
2 -The Piano
3 - The Economist
4 - The Diploma
5 - The Holiday

Series 2 has 7 episodes. It was first aired between 3rd January and the 14th February 1963.

The episodes are:

1 - Wallah-Wallah Catsmeat
2 - The Bath
3 - The Stepmother

4- Sixty-Five Today
5- A Musical Evening
6 - Full House
7 - Is That Your Horse Outside

Series 3 has 7 episodes in it. This series was first shown between the 7th January and the 18th February 1964.

1 - Homes Fit for Heroes
2 - The Wooden Overcoats
3 - The Lead Man Cometh
4 - Steptoe à la Cart
5 - Sunday for Seven Days
6 - The Bonds That Bind Us
7 - The Lodger

Series 4 consists of 7 episodes. It aired between 4th October and 15th November 1965.

1 - And Afterwards At...
2 - Crossed Swords
3 - Those Magnificent Men and Their Heating Machines
4 - The Siege of Steptoe Street
5 - A Box in Town
6 - My Old Man's a Tory
7 - Pilgrim's Progress

Series 5 has 7 episodes. It was aired between 21st February and 3rd April 1970. This was the first series to be shot in colour.

1 - A Death in the Family
2 - A Winter's Tale
3 - Any Old Iron?"
4 - Steptoe and Son — and Son!"
5 - The Colour Problem
6 - T.B. or Not T.B.?"
7 - Men of Property

Series 6 has 8 episodes. It was first aired between 2nd November 1970 and 21st December 1970. This series was again in colour.

1 - Robbery with Violence
2 - Come Dancing
3 - Two's Company
4 - Tea for Two
5 - Without Prejudice
6 - Pot Black
7 - The Three Feathers
8 - Cuckoo in the Nest

Series 7 has 7 episodes. It was first broadcast between 13th February and 26th March 1972.

1 - Men of Letters
2 - A Star Is Born"
3 - Oh, What a Beautiful Mourning
4 - Live Now, P.A.Y.E. Later
5 - Loathe Story
6 - Divided We Stand
7 - The Desperate Hours

Series 8 has 6 episodes. It was shown between 4th September and 10th October 1974.

1 - Back in Fashion
2 - And So to Bed
3 - Porn Yesterday
4 - The Seven Steptoerai
5 - Upstairs, Downstairs, Upstairs, Downstairs
6 - Seance in a Wet Rag and Bone Yard

Two Christmas Specials were made:

The Party, broadcast on 24th December 1974.

A Perfect Christmas, shown on the 26th December 1974.

F

Films

Two Steptoe and Son films were made:

Steptoe and Son (1972)
Steptoe and Son Ride Again (1973)

Steptoe and Son (1972) was written by Galton and Simpson. It was directed by Cliff Owen.

It was distributed by EMI and MGM

The cast is Harry H. Corbett as Harold Steptoe, Wilfrid Brambwell as Albert Steptoe, Carolyn Seymour as Zita, Arthur Howard as Vicar, Victor Maddern as Chauffeur.

Harold and Albert go to a social evening at the local football club which includes a stripper. Harold falls in love with the stripper and they marry.

This is a fairly good film version of the series, one of many cinema spin offs of British television sitcoms in the 1970s.

It is interesting to see the Steptoes house on film with a bigger budget; it creates a bit more realism for the film. The plot is good too with Harold marrying and Albert ruining it for him - even going on his honeymoon with him. This is also the film with the famous scene with Albert bathing in the kitchen sink. Some have suggested that the film is too dark. But as a film version of Steptoe and Son it is relatively successful.

Steptoe and Son Ride Again (1973) was written by Galton and Simpson, and directed by Peter Sykes.

It was distributed by EMI and MGM.

The cast is Harry H. Corbett as Harold Steptoe, Wilfrid Brambell as Albert Steptoe, Henry Woolf as Frankie Barrow, Yooth Joyce as Freda, Milo O'Shea as Dr Popplewell.

The Steptoes have to buy a new horse. Harold gets drunk and spends the money for the horse on a racing greyhound. Harold has bought the horse from a local loan shark Frankie Barrow and now owes him money. The Steptoes decide to fake Albert's death to claim the life insurance on him.

This is another entertaining Steptoe film, which is a little bit lighter than the first one, with lots of farcical moments. It is helped by the fact that the Steptoes are at home more. This has a good supporting cast of popular British actors.

Final Episode

The last episode of Steptoe and Son recorded was A Perfect Christmas, which was recorded on 26th October 1974, and shown on the 26th December 1974.

Foreign Versions

Some other countries made their own versions of Steptoe and Son.

In the US the series was adapted as Sanford and Son, a successful show that ran for 5 series between 1972-77. In this version the two main characters are black junk dealers living in Los Angeles.

In Portugal it was made as Camilio and Filho Lda.

The Netherlands's Steptoe and Son version was Stiefbeen en Zoon which ran for 17 episodes in 1964.

Sweden made a version called Albert & Herbert. This ran from 1974 to 1982 and had the couple living in Gothenburg.

Food

There are many memorable scenes involving food in the Steptoe canon.

Food is used to show when the Steptoes are poor, such as when they only have some cold porridge or tinned snails to eat.

It is also used to show Albert's lack of hygiene and manners, or when he is trying to ruin Harold's relationship with a woman by embarrassing him. For example when he puts the cheese for Harold's cheese sandwich through a mangle to flatten it, scrapes an egg off the floor and puts it back in the frying pan, or crimps the pastry for a pie with his false teeth.

Food shows Albert's selfishness as he often gives Harold a low quality dinner whilst having luxury items such as steak for his meal whilst Harold is working.

Foster

Dudley Foster (1924-1973) was an English actor. He appears in 4 episodes of Steptoe and Son: Robbery with Violence (1970) as The Detective, The Colour Problem (1970) as Car Salesman, My Old Man's a Tory (1965) as Mr. Stonelake, Full House (1963) as Martin

He worked widely in British television in programmes such as Public Eye, Jason King, Armchair Theatre, Z Cars, Doctor Who, The Avengers and Drama 61-67.

His film roles include Moon Zero Two (1962), A Study in Terror (1965), Term of Trial (1962), The Rise and Rise of Michael Rimmer (1970), Follow Me! (1972) and The Little Ones (1965).

He also worked in the theatre.

He died in 1973 aged 48.

Full House

Full House is an episode of Steptoe and Son. It is the 6th episode of series 2. It was first broadcast on the 7th February 1963.

Harold brings some friends back to play cards

at the house. Albert suspects they may be cheats, so sends Harold out to buy some beer and plays them himself.

Also features Dudley Foster as Martin, Jack Rodney as Rex and Anthony Sugar as George.

Harold is again fooled by some people - this time card sharks. But naturally another one of Albert's hidden talents is cheating at cards.

G

Galton and Simpson

Ray Galton OBE (1930-) and Alan Simpson OBE (1929-2017) were the British writers who created and wrote Steptoe and Son.

Galton was born in Paddington in London. Simpson was born in Brixton in London. They had tuberculosis in their youth and were sent in 1947 to Milford Sanatorium in Godalming where they met. They wrote comedy scripts for hospital radio, then got their break when they contributed material to Derek Roy's BBC radio show Happy-Go-Lucky.

Galton and Simpson went on to create the

iconic Steptoe and Son and numerous other comedies such as the ground breaking Hancock's Half Hour radio and television series with Tony Hancock. They contributed material to many comedians and productions.

Their humour is often stated as being somewhat dark in tone.

Simpson retired from writing in 1978 to concentrate on other interests. Galton continued to write scripts, often with Alf Garnett creator Johnny Speight on sitcom such as Spooner's Patch. In 2005 Steptoe and Son in Murder at Oil Drum Lane a play written by Galton and John Antrobus was staged for the first time. Antrobus and Galton also wrote the sanatorium based sitcom Get Well Soon in 1997.

Alan Simpson died on 2017.

Good Luck Scotland

Good Luck Scotland was a BBC Radio 2 show about the Scotland football team in the 1978 World Cup in Argentina. The Steptoes appear in a Galton and Simpson sketch - which has been entitled Scotch on the Rocks - in which Albert says he wishes to go to Argentina to watch the Scotland team play.

Gordon

Colin Gordon (1911-1972) was a British actor. He appears in two episodes of Steptoe and Son: The Holiday (1962) where he plays The Doctor, and Live Now, P.A.Y.E Later (1972) where he plays a tax inspector who visits the Steptoes' house.

His other roles include numerous film appearances such as in The Green Man (1956), The Pink Panther (1963), Heavens Above! (1963)amd Casono Roaye (1967). Television roles include The Baron, Doctor Who, Department S, The Prisoner and Complete and Utter History of Britain.

He often played government officials. A bio states:

"Colin made his mark in the acting profession as much by playing countless supercilious or sneering bureaucrats, lawyers or haughty military types. His stock-in-trade became his ever-present horn-rimmed glasses, combined with a cynical or asinine manner and a precisely modulated voice"

He was born in Ceylon (Sri Lanka).

H

Hayman

Damaris Hayman (1929-) is a British actress. She appears in Seven Days (1964) where she plays a cinema cashier, and My Old Man's A Tory (1965) where she plays Karen Frobisher.

Her film roles include Mutiny on the Buses (1872), The Pink Panther Strikes Again (1976) and The Missionary (1982). Television roles include The Young Ones, Duty Free, The Sweeney, Sez Lez and Doctor Who.

Hayman was born in London, and often plays eccentric upper class roles.

The Holiday

The Holiday is an episode of Steptoe and Son. It was first broadcast on the 12th July 1962. It is the 5th episode in Series 1.

Harold wants a foreign holiday for the first time rather than the usual trip to Bognor

Regis. But Albert does not want to go abroad - so fakes a heart attack.

Colin Gordon appears as the Doctor, and Charlie Bird makes an appearance as a Rock Seller.

The first of several Steptoe episodes where Harold wants a foreign holiday but Albert wants to go to Bognor!

Homes Fit for Heroes

Homes Fit for Heroes is an episode of Steptoe and Son. It is the 1st episode of series 3. It was first broadcast on the 7th January 1964.

Harold plans to be part of a sailing ship exploring the world for two years. He puts Albert in a country old peoples' home.

Also features Peggy Thorpe-Bates as The Matron, Marie Makino as am Old Lady and Molly Veness as a resident of the Old People's Home.

This is a slightly sad episode with Harold planning to put Albert in a home for two years while he goes away. Harold gets his way, but in an ironic twist ending he is not allowed to go on his trip as he is too old!

Howard Davies

John Howard Davies (1939-2011) was a British director and producer who produced and directed series 7 of Steptoe and Son (apart from Divided We Stand).

He was a prolific producer and director of British tv comedy. He produced such shows as Fawlty Towers and The Good Life.

He was Head of Comedy at the BBC from 1977-82, and then Head of Light Entertainment until 1985. He was then Head of Light Entertainment at Thames Television until 1988. He then moved back to the BBC,

He was a child actor appearing in Oliver Twist (1948), The Rocking Horse Winner (1949) and Tom Brown's Schooldays (1951). He is the son of writer Jack Davies.

He died from cancer in 2011.

Hurndall

Richard Hurndall (1910-1984) was a British

actor. He appears in 1 episode of Steptoe and Son, Any Old Iron (1970) where he plays Timothy Stanhope, a gay antiques dealer who takes an interest in Harold.

Hurndall's other work includes Doctor Who in The Five Doctors (1983) where he played the first Doctor (originally played by William Hartnall), The Avengers, Bergerac and Spindoe.

His film roles include Zeppelin (1971), I, Monster (1971), Crossed Swords (1977), Some Girls Do (1969) and Follow That Camel (1967).

He also acted on radio and on stage.

He was born in Darlington. Hurndall died aged 73 in 1984.

I

Is That Your Horse Outside?

Is That Your Horse Outside? is an episode of Steptoe and Son. It is the 7th and last episode of series 2. It was first broadcast on the 14th February 1963.

Harold falls in love with Dorothia, a rich woman who has been separated from her husband for five years. Harold thinks it is serious and she is in love with him, but Albert thinks differently.

Also features Patricia Haines as Dorothia, Richard Shaw as the coalman and Jo Rowbottom.

Harold is again unsuccessful and somewhat naive in his love life.

J

Joyce

Yootha Joyce (1927-1980) was an English actress. She appears in the Steptoe and Son episodes The Bath (1963) and A Box in Town (1965). She also appears in the film Steptoe and Son Ride Again (1973).

She was born as Yootha Joyce Needham in London. Her television roles include BBC sitcom Me Mammy, On the Buses, The Avengers, The Saint and Jason King. Her most famous role was as Mildred Roper in the sitcoms Man About the House and George and

Mildred.

Film roles include Catch Us If You Can (1965), Fragment of Fear (1970), Burke and Hare (1971), A Man for All Seasons (1966) and Charlie Bubbles (1967).

She died aged 53 in 1980.

K

Kneehigh

Kneehigh are a Cornwall based theatre company with a local, national and international profile, creating "vigorous, popular and challenging theatre and perform with joyful anarchy".

The company staged a version of Steptoe and Son in conjunction with the West Yorkshire Playhouse. Adapted & Directed by Emma Rice, it used several of the television series scripts. The plot charted the relationship of the two characters. The play was "designed to highlight the Beckettian nature of Albert and Harold's situation, focusing on themes of over-reliance and being trapped within social class."

It had its first performance in 2012, and has been staged throughout Britain. The play has received positive reviews.

L

Loath Story

Loathe Story is an episode of Steptoe and Son. It is the 5th episode of series 7. It was first broadcast on the 20th March 1972.

Harold loses at badminton to his father, and threatens to join Harold's tennis club. Harold then attempts to kill Albert whilst sleep walking and visits a psychiatrist as a result. At the psychiatrist Harold tells a few anecdotes about his life such as when he was younger, and a recent tale about bringing a posh girlfriend and her mother back to the house to meet his father.

Also features Raymond Huntley as the Psychiatrist, Georgina Cookson as Mre Kennington-Stroud, and Joanna Lumley as Bunty.

This is a nice episode with an interesting flashback of Harold as young boy being left outside on the cart while Albert goes to the pub. It has the familiar tale of Harold bringing a girlfriend back to the house - along with her posh mother - and Albert ruining it with his overly uncouth manners.

The Lead Man Cometh

The Lead Man Cometh is a Steptoe and Son episode. It is the 3rd episode of the 3rd series. It was first broadcast in the 21st January 1964.

The Steptoes' business is not doing well when a suspicious man offers them some cheap lead.

Also stars Leonard Rossiter as Welsh Huhie, the lead seller, and Bill Maxim as a policeman.

A fun episode with a wonderful Leonard Rossiter performance as a con man. Harold is again rather naive in his business dealings.

Live Now, P.A.Y.E. Later

Live Now, P.A.Y.E. Later is an episode of Steptoe and Son. It is the 4th episode of series 7. It was first broadcast in the 13th

March 1972.

Albert has not informed the tax authorities that his wife is dead, and he is still receiving an allowance for her. A tax inspector visits the Steptoes and says that Albert's wife is eligible to receive back pension payments that she has not been claiming. Albert goes to great lengths to pretend his wife is alive so he can get the pension money.

Also features Colin Gordon as Mr Greenwood, Edwin Apps as an official, Peter Madden as Norman, and Carole Roberts.

A memorable and quite farcical episode with the Steptoes dressing up as women to try and fool the social security representatives!

The Lodger

The Lodger is an episode of Steptoe and Son. It was first shown on the 18th February 1964. It is the 7th and final episode of series 3.

Albert advertises for a lodger. Harold moves out in protest.

Also features Walter Swash.

Another episode where Harold moves out of the house and finds another job, but it does not work out for him and he has to move back in with his father and the status quo is renewed.

M

Men of Letters

Men of Letters is an episode of Steptoe and Son. It was first broadcast on the 21st February 1972. It is the 1st episode of series 7.

Harold and Albert are playing Scrabble - Albert is relying on his knowledge of rude words for the game! The vicar asks them to write an article for the 100 years celebration edition of the parish magazine. The Steptoes argue over who will write an article on the rag and bone trade for the magazine. Harold wins the argument and Albert instead comes up with a crossword.

Also stars Anthony Sharp as the Vicar.

Harold fantasises about the opportunity for a new career - this time in journalism. But it is scuppered by Albert as usual, this time with his obscene contribution to the church newsletter. A memorable episode from the later colour series.

Men of Property

Men of Property is an episode of Steptoe and Son. It is the 7th and last episode of series 5. It was first broadcast in the 17th April 1970.

The Steptoes find out that they don't own their house. They have to borrow money from the bank and have to take the bank manager and his wife to an expensive restaurant to win him over.

Also features Norman Bird as the Bank Manager, Hilda Fenemore, Michael Balfour, Peter J. Elliot, Michael Stainton, Tim Buckland, Michael Earl, Peter Thompson, Stella Kimball, Ernest Arnley, Jan Rossini and Walter Swash.

A strange episode this because the Steptoes find out they do not own their own house! They have to wine and dine their bank manager to get a loan to get the lease. As usual Albert embarrasses Harold in the posh restaurant, and it is funny to see the old joke used where Harold has to buy an expensive meal but is trying to keep costs down and is aghast when people keep ordering expensive items. Of course Albert get access to some money at the end and has to spend it again!

Murder at Oil Drum Lane

Murder at Oil Drum Lane is a stage play based on Steptoe and Son. It was written by Ray Galton and John Antrobus, and was first performed in 2005.

In the play it is 2005, and Harold, now in his 70s, visits the Steptoes' old house which is now a National Trust property. Harold states that he killed his father by throwing a spear at him when Albert was using the toilet. Harold has since been living in Rio De Janeiro.

Albert then appears as a ghost and states he is trapped in the house. Then various points in Harold's life are told in flashback.

A Musical Evening

A Musical Evening is an episode of Steptoe and Son. It is episode 5 of the second series.

Harold plans a musical evening after receiving

some old classical records. But Albert plans to mend a collection of old shoes.

A solid farcical Steptoe episode with the pair annoying each other as usual with Albert's work mending shoes ruining Harold's music listening.

My Old Man's a Tory

My Old Man's a Tory is an episode of Steptoe and Son. It was first shown on the 8th November 1965. It is the 6th episode of series 4.

Harold hoped to chosen as the local Labour candidate for the council, He arranges the meeting of the local Labour party at the house. But Albert also attends the meeting, and he is a Conservative supporter.

Also features Dudley Foster as Mr Stonelake, Damaris Hayman, Howard Douglas, Evelyn Lund and Peter Thompson.

A wonderful satiric episode. The Steptoes naturally disagree about politics with Albert being a Conservative and Harold a socialist supporter of the Labour Party. Harold wants to better himself by becoming a Labour candidate for the council, but of course the local Labour candidate feel he is too working class and want a middle class candidate!

N

Nolan

Margaret Nolan (1943) is a British actress. She appears in 1 episode of Steptoe and Son - A Star is Born (1972) as Nemone Wagstaff.

Her television roles include The Saint, Armchair Theatre, The Persuaders, The Sweeney, Q9, Adam Adamant Lives! and Brideshead Revisited.

Her film roles include A Hard Day's Night (1964), Goldfinger (1964), Ferry Cross The Mersey (1965), The Great St Trinian's Train Robbery (1966) and Sky Bandits (1986). She appears in 6 Carry On films Carry On Cowboy (1965), Carry On Henry (1971), Carry On at Your Convenience (1971), Carry On Matron (1972), Carry On Girls (1973), Carry On Dick (1974).

She also appeared on stage.

Nolan started off as a model, and her striking looks saw her cast in numerous productions in the 60s and 70s. She now is now a visual artist. She was born in London.

O

The Offer

The Offer is a television episode of Steptoe and Son.

It was the first episode of the series, and first shown on the 5th January 1962. It was a one-off episode for the Comedy Playhouse series on the BBc. The Comedy Playhouse was a series of one-off sitcoms that ran between 1961-1975 (121 episodes were made). The Comedy Playhouse strand was revived in 2014 and 2016 for 6 more episodes. Many were subsequently turned into series such as Up Pompeii!, Till Death Do Us Part and Last of The Summer Wine.

The Offer introduces Harold and Albert. Harold is 37 years old and has been working with father as a rag and bone man since leaving the army. He gets a good job offer and decides to take it. But Albert tries to get him to stay with him.

Oh, What a Beautiful Mourning

Oh, What a Beautiful Mourning is an episode of Steptoe and Son. It was first broadcast on the 6th March 1972. It is the 3rd episode of series 7.

Albert's eldest brother passes away and the Steptoes attend the funeral with the rest of the Steptoe clan.

Also features George A. Cooper as Uncle Arthur, Mollie Sugden as Auntie Minnie, Rita Webb as Auntie Ada, Yvonne Antrobus as Caroline, Bartlett Mullins as Ted, Tommy Godfrey as Uncle Nobby, Queenie Watts as Joyce, Stella Moray as Elsie, Margaret Flint as Jessie, Simon Cord as Jeffey, Gilly Lower as Alice.

A fun episode - which is also interesting as we get to see Albert's extended family.

Owen

Cliff Owen (1919-94) was a director who directed the Steptoe and Son film Steptoe and

Son (1972).

He was a prolific comedy director the 1960s and 1970s directing such films as Oph...You Are Awful (1972), No Sex Please: We're British (1973), The Magnificent Two (1967), That Riviera Touch (1966) and The Wrong Arm of the Law (1963).

P

The Party

The Party is an episode of Steptoe and Son. It was first broadcast on the 24th December 1973. It is a Christmas special.

Harold pants to spend Christmas in Majorca, but Albert uses his tricks to get him to stay. Harold then decides to throw a Christmas Day party.

Also features Frank Thornton as the Travel Agency Clerk, Arnold Diamond and Mary Barclay as the husband and wife at the travel agency, Peter Hughes, Valeries Bell, Jenny Cox, Peter Thornton, Sue Walker and Shirley Hafey.

This is a wonderful colourful Christmas special with lots of laughs. Harold again wants to go on a foreign holiday, this time over the Christmas period. But Albert does not, so Albert as usual makes Harold feel guilty to get him to stay at the house for Christmas. Harold then throws his party, which goes wrong too - as usual because of Albert! Again in this episode we see Harold being looked down by higher classes - this time in the travel agent.

Pedrick

Gale Pedrick (1906-1970)   was an author, broadcaster, journalist and scriptwriter. He was a script editor and writer for the BBC.

He wrote the novelisations ties in for Steptoe and Son: Steptoe and Son (1964) and Steptoe and Son at the Palace (1966). He wrote the adaptions for the first two series of the Steptoe and Son radio version.

A Perfect Christmas

A Perfect Christmas is an episode of Steptoe and Son. It is a Christmas special and was first aired on the 26th December 1974. It is the last episode of Steptoe and Son.

Harold is determined to go away for Christmas and shows Albert several holiday brochures to choose a destination.

Also features Leon Eagles as Immigration Officer.

Again Harold wants to go away on holiday but Albert is not so keen. This avert good episode, and we learn some information about Albert's family background. Harold even gets a victory in the twist ending where Harold knows his passport has expired and won't be allowed to travel, so Albert goes on the holiday and Harold spends Christmas in Bognor with a girlfriend!

The Piano

The Piano is an episode of Steptoe and Son. It was first broadcast on the 21st June 1962. It is the 2nd episode from Series 1.

Harold has to get a piano from the top floor of a block of flats. He argues with Albert who is helping him, much to the annoyance of the man who is selling the piano.

This episode also features Brian Oulton as the owner of the piano, and Roger Avon as the

Policeman.

A good early episode of Steptoe and Son which has many slapstick elements stemming from the difficulty in removing the piano from a flat.

Pilgrim's Progress

Pilgrim's Progress is the 7th and last episode of series 4 of Steptoe and Son. It was first broadcast on the 15ht November 1965.

Albert is visiting France to revisit the place he fought in World War I. Harold is going too, and Albert gets into arguments with an American and Frenchman on the plane.

Also features Alan Gifford as the American, Frank Thornton as the Frenchman, Sidonie Bond as the Air Stewardess, Fredercick Shiller as the German, Catherina Ferraz and Tim Buckand.

This episode was the last for 5 years before the series returned in 1970. A classic episode in which Albert shows his patriotism arguing with various nationalities about the two world wars on the plane!

Porn Yesterday

Porn Yesterday is an episode of Steptoe and Son. It is the 3rd series of series 8. It was first broadcast on the 18th September 1974.

Harold finds an antique What the Butler Saw film machine complete with a film. But the nude couple in the film are Albert and his sister in law. Harold gives the machine to the vicar for his jumble sale, without the film. But the vicar manages to procure another film - again featuring Albert.

Also features Anthony Sharp as the Vicar, Dorethy Frere as Mrs Cakebread, Joyce Windsor and Gladys, Harry Fielder and Ray Burdis.

A saucy episode and a fun one. Albert was an adult film star in his youth! The vicar is funny too with his eagerness to make money off the machine.

Pot Black

Pot Black is an episode of Steptoe and Son. It was first broadcast on the 7th December 1970. It is the 6th episode in series 6.

Harold buys a snooker table and sets it up in the living room, and then the yard because the table in too big. He challenges Albert to a game and they end up playing in a rainstorm.

Also features George Tovey as a delivery man.

This episode shows the Steptoes again having a battle of wills. Harold wants to be better at something than his father so takes up snooker, but his father is obviously good at the game. It is shame that the colour version of this is missing. Also would the snooker table really be too big for the Steptoes living room?

R

Radio

Steptoe and Son was also made into a radio series.

52 episodes were made, and first aired between 1966 and 1976. They were original adaptions of the television series made especially for radio.

Series 1 and 2 were adapted by Gale Pedrick. The rest of the episodes were adapted by

Galton and Simpson.

Series 1

1 The Offer (3 July 1966)
2 The Bird (10 July 1966)
3 65-Today (17 July 1966)
4 The Stepmother (24 July 1966)
5 The Economist (31 July 1966)
6 Wallah-Wallah Catsmeat (7 August 1966)
7 The Diploma (14 August 1966)
8 Steptoe ala Carte (21 August 1966)
9 The Holiday (28 August 1966)
10 The Bath (4 September 1966)
11 The Lead Man Cometh (11 September 1966)
12 The Musical Evening (18 September 1966)
13 The Bonds That Bind Us (25 September 1966)

Series 2

1 The Siege of Steptoe Street (11 June 1967)
2 Pilgrim's Progress (18 June 1967)
3 The Wooden Overcoats (25 June 1967)
4 Sunday for Seven Days (2 July 1967)
5 The Piano (9 July 1967)
6 My Old Man's a Tory (16 July 1967)
7 Homes Fit for Heroes (23 July 1967)
8 Crossed Swords (30 July 1967)

Series 3

1 A Death in the Family (21 March 1971)
2 Two's Company (28 March 1971)
3 Tea for Two (4 April 1971)
4 T.B. Or Not T.B. (11 April 1971)
5 Without Prejudice (18 April 1971)
6 Cuckoo in the Nest (25 April 1971)
7 Steptoe and Son -and Son (2 May 1971)
8 Robbery with Violence (9 May 1971)

Series 4

1 Full House (30 January 1972)
2 Is That Your Horse Outside? (6 February 1972)
3 The Lodger (13 February 1972)
4 A Box in Town (20 February 1972)
5 The Three Feathers (27 February 1972)
6 The Colour Problem (5 March 1972)
7 And Afterwards At... (12 March 1972)
8 Any Old Iron (19 March 1972)

Series 5

1 The Desperate Hours (26 May 1974)
2 Come Dancing (2 June 1974)
3 A Star is Born (9 June 1974)
4 A Winter's Tale (16 June 1974)
5 Men of Property (23 June 1974)
6 Men of Letters (30 June 1974)

Series 6 and Christmas special

1 Loathe Story (8 February 1976)
2 Oh What a Beautiful Mourning (15 February 1976)
3 Live Now P.A.Y.E. Later (22 February 1976)
4 Upstairs Downstairs, Upstairs Downstairs (29 February 1976)
5 And So to Bed (7 March 1976)
6 Porn Yesterday (14 March 1976)
7 The Seven Steptoerai (21 March 1976)
8 Seance in a Wet Rag and Boneyard (28 March 1976)

Away for Christmas (25 December 1976) (based on 1974 TV Xmas Special)

Rag and Bone Man

A Rag and Bone Man is someone who finds unwanted items and sell them to merchants. Traditionally, Rag and Bone men in Britain would travel around with a bag to put items in. The slightly richer ones would use a cart, sometimes with a pony or horse. Items collected by the men in the past include clothes, scrap metal and furniture.

Rag and Bone men were often those who had fallen on hard times.

The Rag and Bone trade declined in the latter half of the 20th century as specialists took over, and many decided to switch to scrap metal instead.

Remakes

In 2016 the BBC remade a series of lost classic sitcom episodes - of episodes that had been wiped.

A new version of a A Winter's Tale was made. It stars Jeff Rawle as Albert Steptoe and Ed Coleman as Harold Steptoe.

Of course there is a black and white tape version of the 1970 A Winter's tale that is shown on television today, but the original colour version is missing.

Robbery with Violence

Robbery with Violence is an episode of Steptoe and Son. it is the 1st episode of series 6. It was first broadcast on the 2nd November 1970.

Albert knocks over a cabinet containing Harold's porcelain collection. He pretends that the damage was caused by a robbery and the police are called round.

Also stars Dudley Foster as the Police Detective, Edward Evans as the Doctor, Graham Ashley as Assistant Detective, Michael Stainton and James McManus.

A solid episode with Albert again making up a story to solve a problem.

Rossiter

Leonard Rossiter (1926-1984) was an English actor. He appears in two episodes of the series, The Lead Man Cometh (1963), where he plays a man selling suspicious lead, and The Desperate Hours (1972) where he plays an escaped criminal who is stopping at the Steptoes' house.

Rossiter had two famous roles in British television comedy - that of Rigsby in the ITV sitcom Rising Damp, and as Reginald Perrin in the BBC's The Fall and Rise of Reginald Perrin.

His film roles include 2001: A Space Odyssey (1968), This Sporting Life (1963), Barry Lyndon (1975) and The Pink Panther Strikes Again (1976).

He worked extensively in the theatre. He sadly died aged 57 while preparing for a performance of Loot at the Lyric Theatre in London.

Royal Variety Performance

Corbett and Bramble appeared in the 1963 Royal Variety Performance televised on ITV television. They play the Steptoes working outside Buckingham Palace. It was written by Galton and Simpson. A recording still exists, and the audio was released as a single.

S

Seance in a Wet Rag and Bone Yard

Seance in a Wet Rag and Bone Yard is an episode of Steptoe and Son. It is the 6th and last episode of series 8. It was first broadcast on the 10th October 1974.

Albert arrives late one evening and announces that he has been visiting a medium. He arranges a seance with the medium - Madame Fontana - at the house along with a few guests including a widow Dorothy who Albert hopes to marry.

Also features Patricia Routledge as Madame Fontana, Gwen Nelson as Dorothy, Gilly Flower as Mrs Sheldon and David J. Grahame as Mr Sheldon.

A good episode with a mysterious atmosphere and some very amusing lines. Again Albert is planning to marry a woman and things don't go to plan - Dorothy thinks Albert has money and is conning Albert with the medium who is actually her daughter.

The Seven Steptoerai

The Seven Steptoerai is an episode of Steptoe and Son. It is the 4th episode in series 8. It was first broadcast on the 25th September 1974.

Albert is interested in Kung Fu films. When local gangster Frankie Barrow visits the Steptoes and asks for protection money, Albert decides to fight back - he enlists some of his friends to use their marital arts skills!

Also features Henry Woolf as Frankie Barrow, Bill Weston, Stuart Fell, Paddy Ryan and Vic Armstrong.

A fun episode with a martial arts theme - which was popular at the time the episode was filmed with films such as Enter the Dragon. Barrow (who was in Steptoe and Son Ride Again) is menacing, but the spoof martial arts film style fight in the Steptoes' yard is amusing.

Seymour

Carolyn Seymour (1947-) is an English actress who appears in the Steptoe and Son film Steptoe and Son (1972). In the film she plays Zita, a stripper who Harold meets and subsequently marries.

She was born as Carolyn von Benckendorf in Aylesbury in England. Her other roles include the British television series Survivors and Space: 1999; in US television such as Cagney and Lacey, Star Trek: The Next Generation; Magnum P.I. and Quantum Leap.

Her film roles include The Ruling Class (1972), The Bitch (1979), Mortal Kombat: Annihilation (1997) Congo (1995) and Gumshoe (1971).
She has also worked as a voice actress providing voices for video games.

Sharp

Anthony Sharp (1915-1984) was an English actor. He appears in 3 episodes of Steptoe and Son.

The Colour Problem (1970) as The Doctor, Men of Letters (1972) as the Vicar, Porn Yesterday (1974) as Vicar

He had many film and television roles, many as aristocratic types.

His television roles include George and Mildred, The Young Ones, Doomwatch and The Comic Strip. His film roles include Barry Lyndon (1975), Never Say Never Again (1983, A Clockwork Orange (1971) and Black Snake (1973)

He was also a writer, and directed many stage productions.

He was born in London, and died in 1984

Shepherd's Bush

Shepherd's Bush is an area of West London in the London Borough of Hammersmith and Fulham. It is the home of the Steptoes who live on the fictional Oil Drum Lane.

The Siege of Steptoe Street

The Siege of Steptoe Street is an episode of Steptoe and Son. It is the 4th episode of series 4. It was first broadcast on the 25th October 1965.

The Steptoes have a number of bills from various tradesmen they cannot play. These include a bill from a local butcher from whom Albert has been ordering expensive meats and eating them without telling Harold. The tradesmen turn up at the Steptoes' house with some bailiffs.

Also features Robert Dorning, Lane Meddick, Edwin Brown, Bill Maxim, Charlie Bird and Stan Simmons.

A wonderful episode with Albert again proving his penchant for spending sprees, and eating nice food whilst Harold has low quality meals. Albert has another of his fake illnesses.

Sixty-Five Today

Sixty-Five Today is an episode of Steptoe and

Son. It was first shown on the 24th January 1963. It is the 4th episode of series 2.

It is Albert's 65th birthday. Harold broadens Albert's horizons by taking him to the theatre and a Japanese restaurant.

Also stars Frank Thornton as the waiter, Richard Caldocot, Michael Bird, Anthony Chinn, Peter Ching, Myo Toon an Arnan Tokyo.

A solid early episode with Albert showing his uncouthness as usual.

Skeleton

In the Steptoes' lounge they have a skeleton. This as often used as prop by the characters during the series. This was a real skeleton, but several different skeletons were used throughout the series.

Stage

There have been several stage productions of Steptoe and Son.

Steptoe and Son in Murder at Oil Drum Lane

This was first staged in 2005 and was written by Ray Galton and John Antrobus.

Steptoe and Son.

The Engine Shed Theatre Company performed five episodes of the television series in Horsham in 2011. They performed Men Of Letters, Robbery With Violence and Seance in a Wet Rag and Bone Yard and the two Christmas specials.

Steptoe and Son by Kneehigh

Performed first in 2012, this was a play written from several television scripts.

Wilfrid Brambell and Harry H. Corbett performed in a stage version of Steptoe and Son in Australia in 1977.

A Star Is Born

A Star Is Born is an episode of Steptoe and Son. It was first broadcast on the 28th February 1972. It is the 2nd episode of series 7.

Harold joins an amateur dramatic society. The rehearsals are being held at the Steptoes' house.

Also features Trevor Bannister as Rupert Ffaines-Muir, Margaret Nolan as Nemone Wagstaff, Betty-Huntley-Wright as Deirdre, John Quayle, Cy Town and John Anderson.

This is a rather dark episode. Harold is interested in acting and fantasises about being a famous actor. But of course Albert has to ruin it and after being asked to fill in in the stage production is the star of the show whereas Harold's performance is deemed mediocre. Although the episode is funny with the Harold pretensions and Albert's views on the actors, it has a sombre end with Harold telling a young autograph hunter that he is not an actor, just a rag and bone man, and that is what he will always be.

The Stepmother

The Stepmother is an episode of Steptoe and Son. It was first shown on the 17th January 1963. It is the 3rd episode from series 2.

Albert plans to marry a widowed sweet shop owner Emma. Harold is not pleased, and will have to leave the house if the marriage goes ahead. So he tries to make Albert angry -

showing Albert's nasty side - when Emma visits the house.

Also stars Joan Newell as Emma.

Another episode where one of the Steptoes is getting married. This time it is Albert, and Harold has to scupper it.

Steptoe and Son — and Son!

Steptoe and Son — and Son! is an episode of Steptoe and Son. It was first broadcast on the 17th March 1970. It is the 4th episode of series 5.

Pregnant Daphne turns up at the Steptoes and says that Harold is the father of her baby.

Also stars Ann Beach as Daphne and Glynn Edwards as George.

Harold is going to get married again, and has a son. But in this dramatic episode it turns out that it is not Harold's son and a distraught Harold is comforted by Albert.

Steptoe à la Cart

Steptoe à la Cart is a Steptoe and Son episode. It is the 4th episode from series 3. It was first broadcast on the 28th January 1964.

Harold meets a French girl - Monique. He asks her back to the house and Albert likes her - he even speaks French! But it turns out he may have dated her Grandmother....

Also features Frank Thornton as the Butler, Gwendolyn Watts as Monique and Lala Lloyd.

Albert ruins Harold's life again - this time in a rather outlandish way when it becomes apparent that Albert is Harold's French girlfriends Grandfather and Harold's niece! He was with the girl's grandmother during WWI in France.

Languages can be added to Albert's list of skills as it seems he can speak French.

Steptoes

The Steptoes are Albert Steptoe and Harold Steptoe.

Albert Edward Ladysmith Steptoe was born in

1899. He is a veteran of WWI, and with the British Expeditionary Force to Archangel in 1919. His wife Emily died in 1936. He is one of 14 children, and has a daughter in France and a son in Australia. He is patriotic and a Conservative.

He followed in the footsteps of his father to become a rag and bone man.

Harold Albert Kitchener Steptoe was born in 1925 (it was changed to 1930 in the 70s). He served in the army in Malaya (although early episodes suggest he served in the army near the end of WW2). He has followed his father into the rag and bone trade. But he aspires to do something else and escape his working class existence.

Studios

From 1962-1965 Steptoe and Son was filmed at the Lime Grove Studios in Shepherd's Bush in London. The Lime Grove Studios was built in 1915 by the Gaumont Film Company. The BBC then bought it and used it from 1949-1991. Many BBC productions were filmed there. The BBC stopped using it in 1991, and it was demolished in 1993.

From 1970-1974 filming moved to the BBC Television Centre. The BBC Television Centre was in White City in London. Built in 1960 it was the iconic headquarters of BBC television until it closed in 2013. The BBC sold the site and it is being redeveloped to provide housing and other facilities. Some parts of the complex are listed, and the BBC plan to lease back several parts of the complex.

Sunday for Seven Days

Sunday for Seven Days is an episode of Steptoe and Son. It was first shown on the 4th February 1964. It is the 5th episode of series 3.

The Steptoe are going to the cinema, but argue over which film to watch. Harold wants to see Fellini's 8 and a half, Albert prefers Nudes of 1964.

Also features Michael Brennan, Michael Stainton, George Betton, Alec Bregnozi and Kathleen Heath as cinemagoers. Mark Singleton as the cinema manager. Bill Maxim as the Commissionaire. Betty Cardno as the cashier. Katy Cashfield as the Usherette.

A fun episode where Albert's bad behaviour

causes problems at a night out at the cinema.

T

T.B. or Not T.B.?

T.B. or Not T.B.?" is an episode of Steptoe and Son. It was first broadcast on the 10th April 1970, It is the 6th episode in series 5.

Albert is taken to the hospital to have a X-ray to check for tuberculosis. Harold has one too and is found to have TB.

Also features Sidonie Bond and Lala Lloyd as nurses.

Harold thinks he is seriously ill which creates some sad moments. But of course it's a false alarm.

Tea for Two

Tea for Two is an episode of Steptoe and Son. It was first broadcast on the 23rd November 1970. It is the 3rd episode in series 6.

There is a local by-election and Harold and

Albert are supporting opposite sides: Harold Labour, and Albert Conservative. Harold is shocked to hear that the local Conservatives have decided that Conservative Prime Minister Edward Heath should visit the Steptoes' house.

Also stars Geoffrey Chater as Pregrine and Robert Raglan as Mr Caldwell.

Another fun political satire episode with the Steptoes on opposite sides of the political spectrum.

Theme

The Steptoe and Son title music Old Ned was composed by Ron Grainer.

Ron Grainer (1922-1981) was an Australian composer. He moved to London in the 1950s and composed his first famous television theme in 1960 for Maigret. He composed many other television themes as well as scoring numerous films.

One of his iconic themes was the theme to British television series Doctor Who.

Thornton

Frank Thornton (1921-2013) has five guest roles in the television services playing different characters. He appears in the most episodes of Steptoe and Son apart from the two leads.

Thornton was regular in British television comedy. One of his most iconic roles is as Captain Peacock in Are You Being Served?

He also has a role in Steptoe and Son Ride Again (1973) as Mr Russell, a representative of an insurance company.

He has many stage and film roles as well as his television work.

Those Magnificent Men and Their Heating Machines

Those Magnificent Men and Their Heating Machines is an episode of Steptoe and Son. It is the 3rd episode of series 4. It was first shown on the 18th October 1965.

Harold receives some radiators on his round, and decides to fit central heating in the house. He does the job himself, but things do not go to plan.

A good comedy episode with Harold incompetently installing central heating in the Steptoes' house.

The Three Feathers

The Three Feathers is an episode of Steptoe and Son. It is the 7th episode in series 6. It was first broadcast on the 14th December 1970.

Harold buy a Regency commode off a woman at a bargain price. But her husband arrives at the yard offering to buy it back for more money. Harold is then offered even more money for it by an antiques dealer.

Also stars John Arnatt and John Bailey.

A fun farcical episode revolving around Harold's naivete in business as he gets taken in by con men.

Two's Company

Two's Company is an episode of Steptoe and Son. It is the 3rd episode of series 6. It was first broadcast on the 16 November 1970.

Albert reveals that he has asked a woman to marry him. He brings her back to the house and Harold releases that the woman is one of his former lovers.

Also stars Jean Kent as Daphne.

Another episode about one of the Steptoes planning to marry. This time Albert's plans are scuppered because of Harold. Daphne feels she has to leave them both, even though she likes them, and says the Steptoes are "married to each other".

U

Upstairs, Downstairs, Upstairs, Downstairs

Upstairs, Downstairs, Upstairs, Downstairs is an episode of Steptoe and Son. It is the 5th episode in series 8 of Steptoe and Son. It was first broadcast on the 3rd October 1974.

Albert is confined to his bed with a bad back leaving Harold to look after him and do all the chores. As usual Albert takes advantage of Harold.

Also features Robert James as the Doctor.

A wonderful episode with many classic moments - one of the best in the whole series. Harold is tired out having to do all the chores and wait on Albert who is constantly bellowing "Harrolllddd" from upstairs to ask Harold to do things. Albert takes advantage and characteristically does not give Harold credits for his help. And then when his back does go back to normal he pretends to be ill!

W

Wallah-Wallah Catsmeat

Wallah-Wallah Catsmeat is an episode of Steptoe and Son. It was first broadcast on the 3rd January 1963. It is the 1st episode of Series 2.

The Steptoes' horse - Hercules - is ill, Harold becomes depressed, so some fellow rag and bone men help the Steptoes.

This episode also features John Laurie as the Vet, Leslie Dwyer as Lionel Sturgis, George Tovey as a Rag and Bone man and George Betton as Charlie.

A good episode involving the Steptoes' horse Hercules.

When Steptoe Met Son

When Steptoe Met Son is a documentary about the lives of Harry H. Corbett and Wilfrid Brambell. It was made by British channel Channel 4. It was first shown in 2002.

The documentary stated that Corbett and Brambell did not like each other in real life. It said that Corbett was bitter about having to make Steptoe and Son because he could not find other work because he was typecast.

Galton and Simpson refused to take part in the documentary saying that the subject matter was not true. And others - such as family members of the actors - said that the actors did not actually hate each other in real life as the documentary implied.

Wilson

Dennis Wilson (1920-1989) was a British composer.

He composed the incidental music for 28

episodes of Steptoe and Son between 1970 and 1974.

He composed music for numerous television programmes.

He was born in Leicester.

A Winter's Tale

A Winter's Tale is an episode of Steptoe and Son. It was first broadcast on the 13th March 1970. It is the 2nd episode of series 5.

Harold wants to go on a skiing holiday in Austria. Albert is cynical as usual.

In this great episode, Harold wants to go on a holiday, a plot that is used several times in the series.

Wiped

The BBC wiped numerous programmes until 1978 which means that many clips and television shows are not available. In the 50s and 60s the BBC recorded tv on videotape. The tapes were expensive, so they often deleted the tapes and used them again. When colour tv was introduced the tapes were still expensive, so numerous programmes in the early 70s were deleted too.

The 1960s Steptoe and Son episodes were wiped. But they still exist as 16mm telerecordings - My Old Man's A Tory exists as a 405 line reel to reel videotape.

The Colour episodes from series 5 and 6 in 1970 were wiped. But luckily black and white copies using a SV-700 reel to reel video recorder were made for the writes Galton and Simpson by an engineer at the BBC. Only 2 colour episodes from the 1970 series are currently in existence: Come Dancing and Cuckoo in the Nest.

Without Prejudice

Without Prejudice is an episode of Steptoe and Son. It was first broadcast on the 30th November 1970. It is the 5th episode in series 6.

Harold wants to move after a new flyover is built near the house. They view a semi-detached house in a pleasant suburb - but the local Residents' Association do not like the idea of them moving there.

Also features Geral Flood as Estate Agent, Norman Bird as Mr Dyson, Ernest Arnley, Tim Buckland, Philip Howard and Victor Harrington.

A great episode and comment on the class system where the lower class Steptoes appall their potential well to do neighbours. Albert's uncouth behaviour whilst viewing the house provides numerous laughs, and of course he comes up with a cunning way to make money to by asking to be paid by the residents not to move in!

Woolf

Henry Woolf (1930-) is a British actor and theatre director. He appears in The Seven Steptoerai (1974) and the film Steptoe and Son Ride Again (1973) where he plays Frankie Barrow.

His film credits include The Lion in Winter (1968), Alfred the Great (1969) and Gorky Park (1983). TV roles include Rutland Weekend Television, The Sweeney and Doctor Who.

In 1983 he moved with his wife to Canada to teach drama at University. He acted and directed in numerous plays in Britain and north America, and was a friend of Harold Pinter who he frequently worked with.

Wood

Duncan Wood (1925-1997) was a British writer, director and producer.

He produced and directed all the Steptoe and Son episodes in series 1-6.

He was an innovative tv director, directing numerous comedies such as Hancock's Half Hour.

He later became Head of Comedy at the BBC from 1972-73, then worked a Head of Light Entertainment at Yorkshire Television, and subsequently Controller of Entertainment Programmes.

Joe McGrath said of his directing:

"He was carefully selective, knowing exactly the effect for which he was aiming. He was a meticulous planner too - one had to be in those days when programmes and audiences were live. He could judge almost to the second how much audience laughter and reaction time should be added to a script (this was before the laughter was "canned") and knew when additional dialogue and cuts were needed to make up or save time. When directing, everybody knew who was in charge."

The Wooden Overcoats

The Wooden Overcoats is the 2nd Steptoe and Son episode of series 3. It was first broadcast on the 14th January 1964.

Harold comes home with a job lot of coffins. But Albert is spooked.

A good comic episode involving a Harold Steptoe business deal and the Steptoes becoming scared of all the coffins in their house.

Photo Credits

https://commons.wikimedia.org/wiki/File:Rag-and-bone_man,_Streatham,_London,_1985.jpg

12 November 2018

Tony 1212